T0044832

Walt Disney's Lady and the TRAMP

ISBN 0-7935-9615-7

Walt Disney Music Company

DISTRIBUTED BY

HAL·LEONARD®
CORPORATION

7777 W. BLUEMOUND RD. P.O. BOX 13819 MILWAUKEE, WI 53213

Visit Hal Leonard Online at
www.halleonard.com

CONTENTS

Bella Notte
8

Peace on Earth
10

What Is a Baby? / La La Lu
12

The Siamese Cat Song
16

He's a Tramp
18

Lady
20

Bella Notte
(This Is the Night)

Words and Music by PEGGY LEE
and SONNY BURKE

This ____ is the night, ____ it's a beau - - ti - ful night, ____ and we

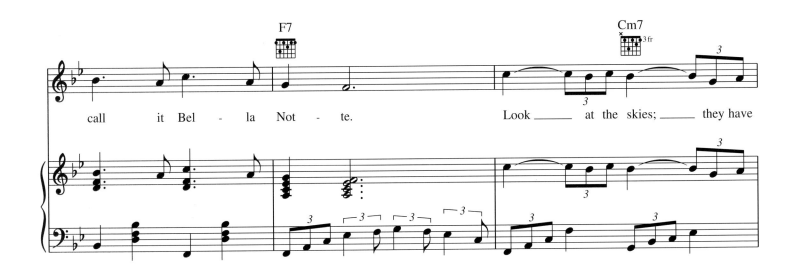

call it Bel - la Not - te. Look ____ at the skies; ____ they have

stars ____ in their eyes ____ on this love - ly Bel - la Not - te. So

9

Peace on Earth
(Silent Night)

Words and Music by PEGGY LEE
and SONNY BURKE

Si - lent as the snow - flake in the night, Ho - ly is the spir - it

of this night, All the world is calm and peace - ful, All the world is

bright and joy - ful, Spir - it of love and

What Is a Baby?/La La Lu

Words and Music by PEGGY LEE
and SONNY BURKE

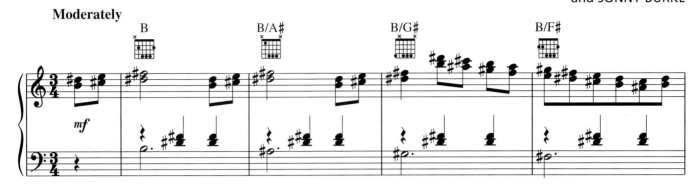

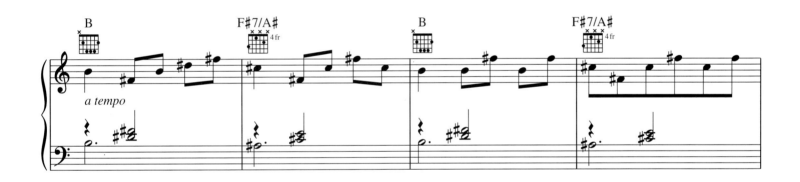

(Spoken:) What is a baby?

The Siamese Cat Song

Words and Music by PEGGY LEE
and SONNY BURKE

He's a Tramp

Words and Music by PEGGY LEE
and SONNY BURKE

8vb

Lady

Words and Music by SIDNEY FINE,
ED PENNER and OLIVER WALLACE